DAVID WILSON, MA, MIFA

MOATED SITES

SHIRE ARCHAEOLOGY

Cover photograph
Little Moreton Hall, near Congleton (Cheshire).
(Photograph: David Wilson.)

British Library Cataloguing in Publication Data
Wilson, David
Moated sites. — (Shire archaeology; 44)
1. Moats — Great Britain 2. Great Britain — Antiquities
I. Title
941 DA90
ISBN 0-85263-756-X

Published by
SHIRE PUBLICATIONS LTD
Cromwell House, Church Street, Princes Risborough,
Aylesbury, Bucks HP17 9AJ, UK

Series Editor: James Dyer

ISBN 0 85263 756 X

First published 1985

Set in 11 point Times and printed in Great Britain by
C.I. Thomas & Sons (Haverfordwest) Ltd,
Press Buildings, Merlins Bridge, Haverfordwest, Dyfed.

Contents

Preface

Moats and their platforms have been the subject of a great deal of interest since the early 1970s, thanks very largely to the influence of the Moated Sites Research Group, the work of whose members, both amateur and professional, has added enormously to the knowledge of these numerous sites. This book is an attempt to bring together the things that have been learnt about moated sites and to discuss some of the problems that these earthworks present. It might also persuade more people to take an active interest in the study and recording of these familiar features of the landscape.

DAVID WILSON
Keele

List of illustrations

Acknowledgements

Many of the figures in this book were originally the work of others and have been previously published elsewhere. The author has redrawn them all, often with amendments or omissions as seemed appropriate to the present purpose, and he would like to acknowledge the following, on whose drawings the figures are based: figs. 4 and 5, A. Oswald; figs. 6 and 20, A. Oswald, G. S. Taylor; fig. 7, J. G. Hurst; fig. 9, C. J. Spurgeon; fig. 10, H. Healey; figs. 11, 13 and 16a, S. E. West; figs. 12, 16c and 17a, G. Beresford; fig. 14, L. Stevens; fig. 15, A. Rogerson, N. Adams; fig. 16b, C. F. Tebbutt, G. T. Rudd, S. Moorhouse; fig. 16d, H. E. J. le Patourel; fig. 17b, H. E. J. le Patourel, P. Wood; fig. 18, D. and D. Miller; fig. 19, Leicestershire Museums Service; fig. 22, C. Hoek.

The author is especially grateful to David Freke and the Liverpool University Rescue Archaeology Unit for providing the original of fig. 3 and for permission to publish; to Alan Aberg for permission to reproduce fig. 8; to Mike Watson for plate 8; to Bob Meeson for plates 13 and 14; to Meridian Airviews for plate 6; to Airviews (Manchester) for plate 10; to the Cambridge University Committee for Aerial Photography for permission to reproduce plates 1 (Crown copyright reserved), 2, 3, 12, 15 and 16; and to the National Monuments Record for permission to reproduce plates 7, 9 and 11.

Finally, the author wishes to thank Vicky Steventon for typing the manuscript and preparing the index.

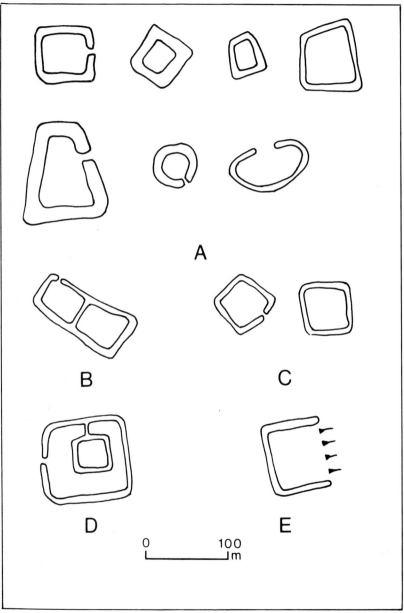

Fig. 1. An indication of the range of moat size and shape (see text for details of types A to E).

1
What is a moated site?

After burial mounds, moated sites are the commonest archaeological field monuments in Britain, numbering at a conservative estimate about five and a half thousand, with a further 750 or so in Ireland. In spite of their being so numerous, or perhaps because they are, it is only comparatively recently that their importance and variety have been fully realised and the sites studied in detail by historians, historical geographers and archaeologists.

No doubt the term 'moat' conjures up in many people's minds a large expanse of water surrounding a majestic castle, and certainly the most impressive moats are of this sort. However, they are few in number compared with the much smaller moats that are associated with more modest structures, and it is with the latter type that this book is concerned.

For general purposes, a moat can be defined as a broad, flat-bottomed or U-shaped ditch, not less than about 4 metres (13 feet) wide and not usually more than 12 metres (40 feet). Moats are most commonly either square or rectangular and less commonly circular, although there are variants, and they were, in the main, originally intended to hold water. Many, however, are today dry or simply boggy. The island or platform around which a moat ran very often, but not always, contained the medieval manor house, although where buildings exist today on platforms they are nearly always of a more recent date. Indeed, many of the complexities of moated site excavation result from the different phases of buildings on the platform. The size of the platform can vary greatly from one site to another. For example, one moated site in Cheshire, known to have had a manor house on it, is about 125 metres (410 feet) long and 75 metres (246 feet) wide, whilst another, also manorial, in the same county, is about 45 metres (148 feet) by 25 metres (82 feet).

Although it was the manor house that was most commonly moated, a wide range of other types of buildings were also surrounded by a moat: for example, monasteries, monastic granges, farmsteads, chapels, medieval hospitals, windmills and so on. In addition, there are a number of examples of moated platforms on which there is no evidence of any building.

Although there are some later ones, the vast majority of

moated sites are of medieval origin, beginning about the middle of the twelfth century and ending about 1500, with a peak in the thirteenth century.

Moats are essentially a lowland feature of Britain and are, in the main, to be found in areas that have a clay subsoil, which can provide water by seepage for the moat and also prevent the water from draining out of the moat.

The functions of moats, as with other aspects already mentioned, will be dealt with in more detail later, but because of the variations in shape, size of platform and type (or lack) of building on the platform it would be very unwise to assume that all moats performed an identical function. Furthermore, moated sites should not be seen as isolated features somehow divorced from the surrounding landscape; each moat was simply part of a much larger medieval complex. Also, the buildings that stood on the platform were, in most cases, the same as hundreds of other medieval buildings up and down Britain. Usually the only distinguishing feature was the moat itself.

Plate 1. Linwood (Lincolnshire): two unlinked moats lying side by side.

2
Classification of moated sites

When any type of archaeological monument or artefact exists in considerable numbers, it is frequently necessary to classify the material in order to determine the differences that occur within the overall type and to assess their significance. The main classifications of moated sites in terms of their physical properties are based upon shape, size, siting and platform height.

Shape and size

The range of variation in these two aspects is indicated in fig. 1. There are firstly what could be described as 'simple' shapes (A): square, rectangular and circular moats, of varying sizes. The square and rectangular moats are the commonest throughout Britain. For example, out of 107 moated sites in Shropshire, eighty-two fall into these categories; in Worcestershire the figure is ninety out of 146, and the twenty moated sites so far recognised in Northumberland are all rectangular, as are the seventeen sites in Glamorgan. Although figures do vary from county to county, there is a clear preference for moats of these shapes. Circular or penannular moats are far less common. In Yorkshire, for example, only half a dozen or so are circular, out of a total of over three hundred moats in the county; in Essex the proportion is even smaller, with eight out of over five hundred; in Worcestershire nine out of the total of 146 are circular or oval, whilst of the 130 or so moats in Wales, six are circular.

A more complex type is that which we can call the double moat (B in fig. 1), where two platforms exist side by side, separated by one line of the moat and enclosed by the other four sides, one perhaps having been occupied by a house and the other by outbuildings or gardens. Although they are far less numerous than the single square or rectangular moats, their frequency varies from county to county. For example, in Shropshire there appear to be none, while in Yorkshire there are over forty. A variation of this type (plate 1 and C in fig. 1) is where two unlinked moats lie close to each other. Another type of double moat (D in fig. 1) is that where one moat lies within another, either separate or linked. These again form a very small proportion of the total number within any county; there are a couple in Cheshire (plate 2) and in Shropshire, for example, and fewer than twenty in Yorkshire.

There are, in addition to the above, moats of irregular shape that do not lend themselves to any classification and are relatively few in number. One oddity in moat shape, however, does stand out and that is the three-sided or even two-sided moat (E in fig. 1). If defence or security was a consideration in the construction of a moated site, then a three-sided moat would seem to be particularly ineffectual. It may be that in some cases the moat was never finished, or that the lie of the land was such that a fourth side was not needed for defence, or that, as in the case with a three-sided sixteenth-century moat at Haslingfield Hall (Cambridgeshire), it was a late ornamental moat. It is sometimes thought that three-sided moats are usually post-medieval, but in the old county of Yorkshire, at least, where there are more than a dozen such moats, they are mainly medieval and one of them, at Low Catton (now in Humberside), has thirteenth-century documentary evidence for the existence of only three sides. But this type of moat demonstrates the inherent danger of classification according to shape: the shape that a moat has today may well be different from that which it had originally. Indeed, it might have changed its shape a number of times over the centuries as a result of infilling and recutting, and so, for example, many three-sided moats could have originally had four sides, one of which has since been filled in and can now only be traced by geophysical survey, aerial photography or excavation.

The significance of the shape of a moat is uncertain, but limited excavation evidence suggests that round moats were among the earliest to have been constructed.

As the shape can vary from one moat to another, so can the size. In Shropshire, for example, all but five of the moats surround a platform which is 0.4 hectare (1 acre) or less in area; in Essex the platforms vary from 20 metres (66 feet) square to nearly 6 hectares (15 acres), with the most common size being 0.2 to 0.4 hectare (½ to 1 acre); in south Lancashire forty-six out of the fifty measurable moated sites have platforms of 0.2 hectare (½ acre) or less; in west Suffolk seventy-four out of 106 sites are 0.2 hectare (½ acre) or less, and eleven are more than 0.5 hectare (1¼ acres); in Worcestershire fifty per cent of the moats have platforms of 0.4 hectare (1 acre) or less, and twenty-five per cent of 0.4 to 0.8 hectare (1 to 2 acres); in Cambridgeshire they range from a few metres square up to 2 hectares (5 acres). These variations in size are significant in terms of the structures which existed on the platform. For example, a large platform would probably have contained a larger number of buildings than a

Plate 2. Concentric moats at Minshull Vernon (Cheshire).

Plate 3. Eaton Bray (Bedfordshire). An originally circular moat recut to be rectangular.

smaller. On the smallest sites, which are sometimes less than 20 metres (66 feet) square, there might simply have been a windmill on the platform, but on the largest ones there would have been a hall, a chapel, various outbuildings, gardens and possibly a pond. In between these extremes, the average-sized platform would have supported a domestic building with perhaps an ancillary building or two. In addition, there might be a correlation between the size of a moated platform and the social status of the medieval owner. For example, the four largest platforms in south Lancashire, each of which was more than 0.25 hectare (⅔ acre) in area, were owned by particularly wealthy families. However, the evidence for this correlation generally is far from conclusive.

A number of moats have been shown to have changed both their size and shape during their history. For example, Moat House, Longnor (Shropshire) had its moat widened by 3.6 metres (12 feet) between 1291 and 1298; the rectangular moat at Wexham Court (Berkshire) was possibly recut in the thirteenth century from an earlier circular moat and a similar recutting from circular to rectangular can be seen at Eaton Bray (Bedfordshire; plate 3); at the Manor of the More, Rickmansworth (Hertfordshire), the double-moated enclosure of the thirteenth century was converted to a single moat between 1300 and 1350, and then, sometime after 1426, a completely new moat was dug. More recent changes took place at Bradwell Bury (Berkshire), where the medieval platform of 115 metres (377 feet) by 50 metres (164 feet) was reduced in size sometime after the sixteenth century to 49 metres (161 feet) by 55 metres (180 feet) as a result of recutting and backfilling and at Brand Hall (Shropshire), where the moat was narrowed in the eighteenth or nineteenth century when the platform became a formal garden.

Siting
This method of classification is based upon the topographical position of the moat, and three main positions have been suggested. First is the *level moat*, which is sited on level ground and whose original water supply was obtained by springs and seepage. Second is the *perched moat*, so called because it sits on a valley side, obtaining its water by seepage or by means of artificial watercourses, called leats, joined to nearby streams. Third is the *valley moat*, which is sited in the bottom of the valley and whose water is provided by a stream running through or adjacent to the moat.

As with virtually every other aspect of moated sites, there is no

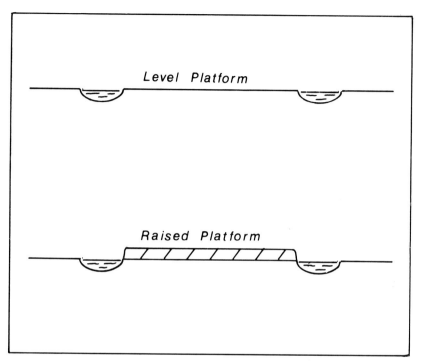

Fig. 2. Profiles of level and raised platforms.

uniformity in their siting. In Cheshire and Shropshire, for example, the siting is predominantly level, about three-quarters of the moats in the latter county being so sited; in Worcestershire about half of the total are level and a third are valley moats. But in Cambridgeshire, by contrast, nearly three-quarters are valley moats, and only about one-tenth level.

Whether the topographical siting of a moat had any significance other than convenience is unknown, but it often appears that there was a definite desire to take water to the moat rather than to lead it away.

However, factors other than the topographical position could determine the siting of a moat, such as the geology of the area, the availability of water, the existing and previous settlement pattern, and perhaps simply the personal preferences of the landowner. The answers can only be found through a knowledge of local conditions.

Plate 4. Raised platform at Foxtwist, near Macclesfield (Cheshire).

Platform height

The final method of classification relates to the platforms, which fall into two types: those platforms whose surfaces are level with the land outside the moat, and those whose surfaces are raised above the level of the surrounding area (fig. 2). In the case of the latter, the raising has been brought about by depositing the upcast from the moat digging on to the internal area (see plate 4). Where the platform is level with the surrounding area the upcast was presumably carted away and deposited on the fields, or used in constructing banks on the perimeter of the platform or on the outer side of the moat.

Raised-platform sites are less common than level platforms. They are very rare, for example, in Cambridgeshire and there are fewer than one in ten in Yorkshire. However, the number is greater in Shropshire, about a quarter, and in Norfolk a high proportion of the platforms is raised.

It is possible that the raised platform was, in some cases, a copying of the motte of a motte and bailey castle, but in other cases it may well have been a safety precaution against the moat flooding, a means of covering previous settlement material and providing a new building surface, or simply the result of putting the moat upcast in the handiest place.

To the archaeologist, however, one importance of this classification according to platform height is the potential dating evidence to be obtained from a raised platform. Where documentary evidence is lacking, it is usually only a raised platform that can be used to date the cutting of a moat, either because the upcast on the platform seals pre-moat occupation material, the dates of which can be compared with those of material on the top of the platform, or because as there can have been no pre-moat occupation *on top* of the raised platform, the earliest-dated material from the top is likely to date the cutting of the moat. The dating of moats is discussed more fully later.

A second way in which the raised platform is important to the archaeologist is that, because it seals the pre-moat ground surface, it is also sealing environmental material, pollen for example, which can tell us a great deal about the vegetation and climate up to the time of the moat cutting.

Fig. 3. Suggested reconstruction of the wooden medieval bridge remains found during excavation at Twiss Green, Culcheth (Cheshire).

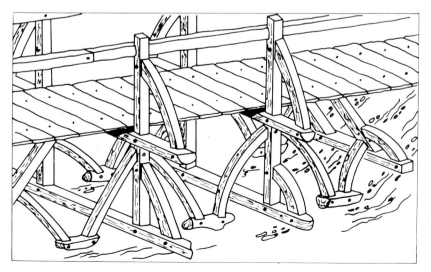

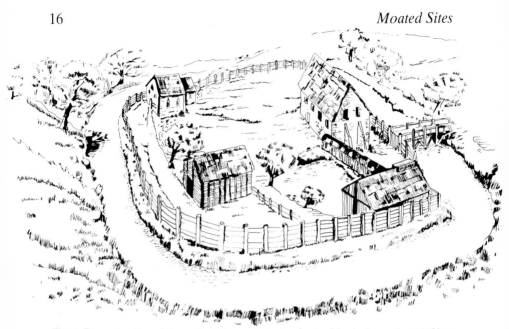

Fig. 4. Reconstruction of the earliest phase of Weoley Castle, Birmingham, about 1150 to 1260.

Fig. 5. Ground plan of Weoley Castle, Birmingham, after it had obtained a licence to crenellate in 1264.

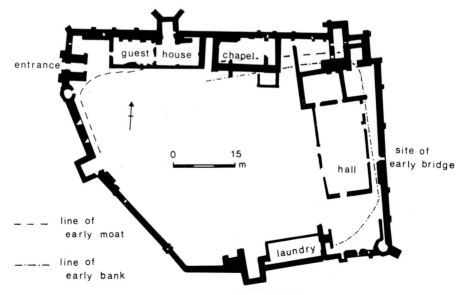

3
The functions of moats

When looking at the large moat of a castle, there is no doubt that it forms part of an often elaborate defensive system, preventing a frontal assault and keeping would-be attackers at bay. However, it is impossible to make a simple, general statement about the function of the sort of moat that this book is concerned with as that of one moat might well not be the same as that of another. A number of reasons have been suggested for the cutting of moats, and these will be considered in turn.

Defence

By analogy, again, with the castle, the obvious reply to the question 'Why dig a moat?' would be 'To provide a means of defence'. There is much truth in this, but the meaning of 'defence' needs to be looked at more closely. The vast majority of moats are far too small to provide any sort of defence against large groups of armed men intent on the destruction of the site, in spite of the popular belief that the moats of some counties, Cheshire for example, were dug to keep out hordes of marauding Welshmen! In reality a moat would provide security, rather than defence, deterring thieves and cut-throats at a time when there was considerable lawlessness in the countryside, and when feuding between families was far from unknown. But these conditions did not pertain constantly during the 350 years or so of moat building, and there were times when the need for the security of the moat would have been greater than at others. The fact that at least some moated sites have been shown, by excavation or documentation, to have had drawbridges also suggests the element of security.

Only on a very limited number of sites have the remains of original bridges been found. These include Bushwood Hall, Lapworth (Warwickshire), where mechanical cleaning out of the moat exposed the support timbers and central stone pier of a massive oak drawbridge which had been buried in a later entrance causeway; Acton Burnell (Shropshire), where the support timbers of a possible drawbridge of the late thirteenth century were excavated; and an example found during excavation at Twiss Green, Culcheth (Cheshire; fig. 3). Documented bridges are not uncommon: for example, a site at Allexton (Leicestershire) is described in 1297 as 'surrounded with a moat and water, which could not be entered without forcing the bridges and doors'; Birmingham Manor is recorded as having a drawbridge in 1529; in a record of expenses of 1290 for Prestbury Moat (Gloucestershire) is included the cost of repairing a turning bridge; and in the later fourteenth century new drawbridges were put over the moat at Byfleet (Surrey).

A problem arises with those moats which today have a fixed means of access to the platform, such as a causeway or a stone bridge. If these features are original, then it is difficult to see such sites as being very secure. Excavation can show whether or not the causeway was there from the time of the moat digging. At the author's excavation of a site at Buttery House Lane, Hale Barns, Manchester, the causeway was clearly not original as it overlay moat silt and was dated by modern coins at its base; on the other hand, at Hawkesley Farm, Longbridge, Birmingham, it was shown that the causeway was an original feature of the site, as it was also at Huttons Ambo, near Malton (North Yorkshire), where the moat was interrupted by a causeway of solid rock, the entrance over which was controlled by a large gateway, although this must have provided less security than a drawbridge. Many of the stone bridges across moats are medieval, as for example at Hulme Hall, Allostock (Cheshire; plate 5), but again excavation, together with documentary evidence, can often tell us if the bridge replaced an earlier means of access.

Some moated sites were potentially more 'defensive' than others, notably those that obtained a licence to fortify by means of crenellation (the putting up of stone walls, battlements, towers and such like). For example Weoley Castle, Birmingham, began in about 1150-1260 as a stone dwelling house with wooden outbuildings surrounded simply by a ditch and palisaded bank (fig. 4). In 1264 it obtained a licence to crenellate, and shortly afterwards the present moat was dug and stone walls and towers were erected, making it much more defensively impressive (fig. 5). However, there is no necessary connection between licences to crenellate and moated sites, as many unmoated structures had such licences, and it may be that the desire to give a more impressive appearance to one's home, rather than actually to make it more defensive, was often the reason for the petition for the licence.

Some sites that were never crenellated do seem to have increased their defensive potential from time to time. At Shareshill (Staffordshire) in the twelfth century there was an enclosure surrounded by a ditch with an internal bank fronted by

Plate 5. Medieval bridge across the moat at Hulme Hall, Allostock (Cheshire).

a timber fence, but in the thirteenth century the moat was enlarged and a new internal bank was put up, probably topped by a sandstone wall, outside of which there may have been a thorn hedge. Again, at Huttons Ambo (North Yorkshire) a triangular enclosure of the twelfth century, surrounded by a bank and ditch too small to be defensive, was extended by the digging of a larger moat, some 4.5 metres (15 feet) wide and 4 metres (13 feet) deep. But it would be wrong to assume that there was a universal increase in the defensive nature of moated/ditched sites; it would also be wrong to assume that changes, even enlargements, necessarily increased the defensive properties of a site. For example, at Durrance Moat, Upton Warren (Hereford and Worcester), there was a thirteenth-century enclosure surrounded by a V-shaped ditch and a large clay, timber-laced bank or rampart. In the fourteenth century the ditch was enlarged and the upcast spread over the old site, but no bank or rampart replaced the old one, so it could be said that the defences were now weaker, in spite of the enlarged moat (fig. 6). Internal and external banks and palisades are discussed again later.

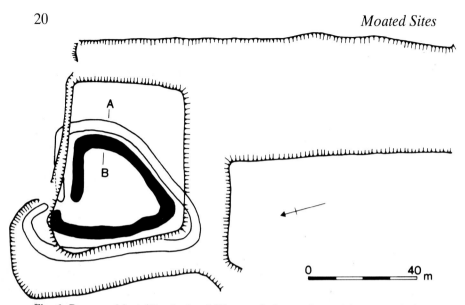

Fig. 6. Durrance Moat (Hereford and Worcester). Larger fourteenth-century platform and moat overlying and cutting the thirteenth-century ditch (A) and bank (B).

It has been suggested that moats were intended to provide protection not against people but against wild animals intent on attacking the domestic animals on the site. But we should beware of overestimating the number of wild animals roaming the countryside in the middle ages, and many moated platforms are so small that it would have been impossible for them to have accommodated the domestic animals. On the other hand, the moat would serve to keep out herbivorous animals, such as deer, which might damage domestic gardens, and this might well be the reason for the existence of certain moats, such as that at Slipton Lodge, Lowick (Northamptonshire), which is the site of the medieval deer-park keeper's lodge and lies within the park itself.

There is a third agent against which a moat can be considered as providing protection, and that is fire, and this may well have been an incentive to moat digging, especially in places adjacent to woodland, where the moat could act as a firebreak and as a source of water for putting out a fire. Indeed, in a period when so many buildings were of timber, the danger of fire was ever present, and a moat full of water must have been a comforting sight, even if fire-fighting was not its major function.

Drainage

As the vast majority of moated sites are to be found in badly drained areas, such as those where the drift geology is predominantly clay, it would seem not unreasonable to view the moat as basically a drainage ditch, carrying water from the platform and hence creating a drier place for habitation. However, it is most likely that a clay area was chosen for the moat digging precisely *because* it was wet and would readily provide water for the moat, with the clay itself giving stable sides to contain this water. Further, it seems extremely unlikely that artificial watercourses would be created to carry water *into* moats, as we not uncommonly find, if the function of the moat was to take water *from* the platform. Again, it is difficult to explain in terms of drainage those moats which were dug in better drained areas and had to be lined with clay in order to prevent the water seeping away. At Weoley Castle, Birmingham, for example, the subsoil is a highly porous red sandstone, and as a result the moat was lined with puddled clay; excavation showed that there were six layers of this puddled clay, so it would seem that this lining had to be replaced from time to time, presumably after the cleaning out of the moat. Finally, there seems to be little correlation between the period of intensive moat digging and that of very wet weather conditions.

All of this does not preclude the possiblity that on some sites the moat might have helped in the general drainage, but it does indicate that this is extremely unlikely to be its primary function.

Use as a fishpond

Fishponds, often associated with manorial sites, were a common feature of the medieval landscape and bear witness to the importance of fish in the medieval diet. However, it is very unlikely that a moat would have been dug specifically to house fish, when a less complex pond could have been made more easily. This is not to suggest that moats, once dug, were not used as fishponds in addition to their other functions; indeed it would be surprising if they had not been, and it is not unusual to find documentary evidence for this. For example, in 1282 the fish in the double moat of Baynard Castle in Humberside were valued at 66s 8d, and in 1367 a tenant of a moated site at Cowick (Humberside) was brought before the court for poaching roach and pickerel from the moat. Sometimes appearances can be deceptive and a rectangular layout of fishponds can give the impression of a moat, as at Old Madeley Manor in Staffordshire (see plate 6), where the fishponds are adjacent to a genuine moat and enclose the site of a garden.

A source of fresh water

When one looks today at deserted moated sites with their often stagnant water it is difficult to imagine the moats once providing fresh water for the inhabitants of the platform. Doubtless regular cleaning out of the moat in the medieval period would have kept the water cleaner, but the evidence that we have for the latrine emptying into the moat suggests that the water could have been far from fresh. On the other hand, there is not always evidence, from either documents or excavation, of early wells within moated enclosures, although the author's excavation at Cold Norton, Stone (Staffordshire), exposed two fine, stone-lined wells, possibly medieval although the dating is as yet uncertain. So it may be that on occasions the moat might have provided water for consumption, although it is hardly likely that it would have been dug solely for that purpose.

Social prestige

A popular view of the function of moats is that they were dug in imitation of the great castle moats, to emphasise and enhance the social standing of the people living on the platform. In very many instances moats enclosed manor houses and were consequently associated with families of importance and they may sometimes have been dug to make this importance very clear. For example, a study of the size and distribution of moated sites in Cambridgeshire has produced evidence to suggest that social prestige might have been important. In the outlying, remoter areas of the west and south-east of the county, where we might expect large moats to provide defence for buildings and animals, we find small moats, whilst in the other parts of the county, within large villages, where the need for defence was presumably less, we find large, elaborate moated sites. The inference to be drawn from this is that defence was not an overriding consideration, and that the social aspect was at least as important.

There are also examples of the rise in fortune of a family coinciding with the construction of a moat around its house, which suggests a desire to show off. However, it may be that, once the family had acquired the sort of wealth that raised it socially, it *needed* the moat as security against thieves, whereas it had not previously. So it is difficult to be sure in such cases whether it was necessity or vanity that was the prime mover, although the possibility that vogue played its part should not be discounted: once, for whatever reason, moating had begun, it could have become fashionable. An interesting line of enquiry

Plate 6. Moat and fishponds at Old Madeley Manor (Staffordshire).

which is being followed is why some families of considerable social standing had moats and others of equal standing did not, despite appropriate factors such as geology and topography.

These, then, are some of the answers to the problems of the functions of moats. Whatever its ancillary uses, the moat was basically a provider of security to those on the platform, but it is only by looking at local conditions, geographical, historical, social and economic, together with dating evidence, that we can begin to be confident about the function of any given moat.

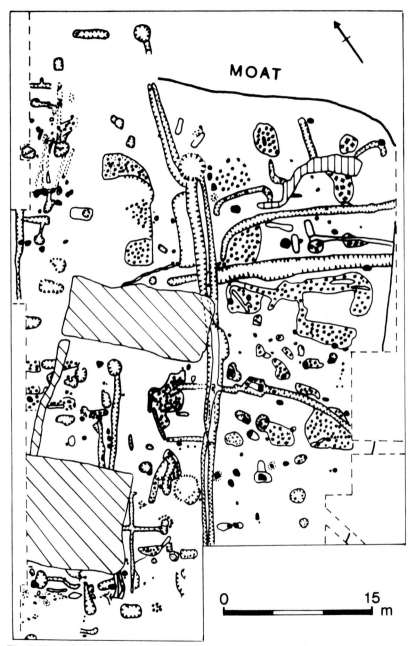

MOAT

0   15
m

Fig. 7. Northolt (Greater London): AD 600-1300. Plan of the excavated area containing Saxon graves, a complex sequence of timber buildings and drainage ditches, cut by a fourteenth-century moat and sealed by its upcast.

4
Dating of moats

There are two potential sources of evidence for the dating of the cutting of moats: documents and excavation. Unfortunately, neither provides this evidence as often as one would hope or perhaps expect.

Documents

As far as the historian is concerned, it is a pity that a licence was not required to dig a moat as it was to crenellate; if it had been, then a written record would exist of the date of the digging. On occasions, however, it is possible to associate the digging or alteration of a moat with the granting of a licence to crenellate. The owners of the Manor of the More, Rickmansworth (Hertfordshire), for example, were granted a licence in 1426 to 'enclose, crenellate, enturret and embattle with stones, lime and brik their manor . . .', and excavation has shown that the cutting of a new moat around the manor house dates from 1426 onwards. Similarly, a licence to 'enclose with a ditch and a wall of stone and lime, fortify and crenellate the dwelling house of . . . Weoley', was granted in 1264 to what is now known as Weoley Castle, Birmingham. The licence in this case is explicit about the 'ditch', and from excavation the construction of the present moat (replacing an earlier palisaded bank and ditch), together with outer walls and curtain towers, can be dated to 1270-80. A third and very late example is that of the 'castle' at Kirby Muxloe (Leicestershire; plate 7), which received its licence in 1474. The raising of the fortified manor house and the digging of the moat were begun in 1480 and are recorded in detail in the contemporary building accounts. In order to carry out the work extra labour had to be brought on to the estate, and eventually eleven men were working four days a week on the digging of the moat alone. These three examples also illustrate the way that documentary work and excavation can and should go hand in glove. Very occasionally we come across references to actual moat construction. For example, at Brill (Buckinghamshire) the accounts for 1181-2 contain reference to a master *fossator* or ditcher and others who were employed in surrounding a new royal chamber with a ditch and bank; the household accounts of 1323 for the manor of Cowick (Humberside) record the digging of a great ditch 40 feet (12 metres) wide and 10 feet (3 metres) deep; and

Plate 7. Kirby Muxloe (Leicestershire).

contemporary documents record that in 1375 at Beckley (Oxfordshire) the great moat around a royal hunting lodge was drained so that building could be carried out in it, and whilst this was going on an outer moat was dug. Usually, however, we have to rely on incidental references to moats in manorial records, which in the main are concerned with matters relating to already existing moats. For example, the account roll of 1324/5 for the manor of Downton (Wiltshire) records the making of an enclosure around *la Mote,* and also an income of 12d from selling the pasture in *la Mote.* Again, in a document of 1355, we are told that at Knutsford Booths (Cheshire) the *lake* around the manor house was worth 12d, presumably because of the fish in it. Sometimes, as will be seen in more detail in chapter 6, there are medieval records listing the buildings and appurtenances on the platform, but these, like so many of the other documentary references, merely indicate to us that a moat existed at the time of the writing of the document.

Excavation

It might seem reasonable to suppose that any datable material excavated from the lowest silt of a now dry moat would date the original digging of the moat. Unfortunately, because of the medieval practice of regularly cleaning out the moats very thoroughly, the material will date from the last cleaning, rather than the original digging, and consequently, if we relied on this dating evidence alone, we would often assign moats to the seventeenth or eighteenth century rather than to the medieval period.

If the moat cannot help in dating its own cutting, then we must turn to the platform. And here again we must beware of making assumptions that may not be true. For example, if the excavated material from the platform dates back to the thirteenth century, it does not necessarily indicate that the moat was dug in the thirteenth century; it depends upon the type of platform. If it is *level*, then the evidence from excavation may give the date of the earliest occupation of the site, rather than the cutting of the moat, because the platform area could have been occupied for some time before it was decided to have a moat around it.

There is much greater certainty when the platform is *raised*, whether or not there was previous occupation of the site. The raising was carried out by throwing the upcast from the moat digging into the central area, so making it up to as much as 2 metres (7 feet) higher than the land outside the moat. Consequently, the 'new' platform must date from the cutting of the moat, and so the earliest material found from its excavation should date the creation of the moat. If the site had been previously occupied, and the buildings levelled immediately before moating, the raised platform would seal the occupation material, the latest of which could be compared with the earliest of the material from the new settlement on the raised platform. If the two correlate, then we have a double check on the dating of the moat; if they do not, then we have an indication of the time lag between the disuse of the first settlement and the cutting of the moat.

At Milton (Hampshire) evidence of three phases of occupation was found under the raised platform, ending well into the thirteenth century, and the earliest material on top of this platform, and hence dating the moat, was fourteenth-century. Excavation of Westbury Moat, Ashwell (Hertfordshire), showed that the remains of timber buildings of the twelfth and thirteenth centuries had been sealed by the upcast of fourteenth-century moat digging, whilst at Northolt (Greater London; fig. 7) there was evidence of a complex series of timber buildings dating from the eighth to the thirteenth century, similarly sealed in the fourteenth century. A very close correlation between the date of the disuse of the pre-moat settlement and the digging of the moat was found at Wintringham (Cambridgeshire), where pottery dating from about 1175-1250 was found in association with two houses, sealed by upcast, whilst the first house to be built on top of the upcast could be dated to about 1250.

At these sites it was possible to get accurate dating, but it is often very difficult and sometimes impossible to date medieval pottery, the major evidence, with precision. As a result, the dating of phases of activity on sites is frequently tenuous. One reason for the importance of dating the cutting of a moat is that it might tell us something of the moat's function. For example, as we have seen, the moat has sometimes coincided with the social rise of a family, suggesting either that it was to provide security or to impress, and it may be that other moats can be shown to have been dug at times of lawlessness in the area, or of woodland clearance, or of local feuding, and so on. In addition, in the case of a village which possesses more than one moat, dating can show whether the moats were contemporary, possibly indicating that there was more than one manor or sub-manor, or whether they were constructed at different times without any overlap of occupation, suggesting that an earlier moated manor house had been moved to a new site in a different part of the village.

From the limited dating evidence that we have, it seems that moating began about 1150, with an initial phase lasting fifty years or so, when probably fewer than a thousand moats were dug. The most prolific moat digging took place during the thirteenth century and the early part of the fourteenth, when some three and a half thousand moats were constructed, after which, up to about 1500, about six or seven hundred moats were dug.

From the beginning of the sixteenth century moats go out of vogue, and any new ones tend to be 'imitation' moats, usually landscaped garden features such as at Snape Wood, Bulwell (Nottinghamshire), where a moat with external banks was dated by botanical and ceramic evidence to between 1855 and 1870, the platform having been used as a garden and the moat possibly having a drainage function, and at Hamerton (Cambridgeshire), where a seventeenth-century moat was part of an elaborate garden system associated with a manor house. Out of sixty-three moated sites examined in west Cambridgeshire, seven proved to be post-medieval gardens, ranging in date from the sixteenth to the nineteenth century.

5
Distribution and location

The national distribution of moats is shown in fig. 8, and from this and from more localised distributional studies a number of facts emerge: there are concentrations of moats in particular areas, for example the Suffolk, Essex, Hertfordshire region and the central Midlands; moats are generally associated with lowland areas; these lowland areas have, in the main, a clay subsoil. In addition, high numbers of moats seem to occur in places that were assarted, that is colonised from woodland, during the thirteenth and fourteenth centuries. In these colonised places the normally tight medieval restrictions of land tenure tended to become slacker than elsewhere and, from research carried out on the Arden area of Warwickshire, it appears that quite small landowners were constructing their moats. In Cheshire, however, the laws of the medieval royal forest were very strict, and moats are conspicuously absent in such forest areas. In Wales, most moats are found in the eastern lowlands on the border with England and along the southern seaboard (fig. 9), and it is not surprising to find that the vast majority of them were manorial and owned by Englishmen.

The picture presented in fig. 8 inevitably masks, because of its scale, local aspects of distribution. Just as the national distribution can be affected by such factors as geology and altitude, so can the distribution within a county. In Cheshire again, for example, there are areas in the centre and the east of the county where there are virtually no moats, because the central sandstone ridge and the Pennine foothills are geologically unsuitable. Similarly, few moated sites are found on the sandstone hills of north Worcestershire or on the chalk downlands of Hampshire.

Another aspect of particular significance at this local level is the siting of moats in relation to settlements, existing or deserted, whereby a moat can either be within a settlement or in an isolated position more than 800 metres (½ mile) from a settlement or parish church. For example, in the reorganised county of Somerset, eleven out of the thirty-two moats are isolated, in Cambridgeshire thirty-five out of over 170 are isolated, in Shropshire seventy-one out of 107, and in Worcestershire eighty-three out of 146. The usual explanation for such isolated moats is that they are associated with the process of assarting and that they surrounded the new farmsteads of the small landowners carrying out the colonising. This view has been supported by a number of pieces of research, particularly in the West Midlands. Those moats lying within settlements have generally been considered as surrounding the manor house of the settlement, and so differing in origin and social standing from the isolated sites. In the majority of cases, these explanations are probably valid, although it is perfectly possible to find manorial moats in isolated situations and non-manorial moats within settlements.

When moats are studied in relation to their position *within* a settlement, they are seen to occupy one of three basic locations: either central, or between the centre and the boundary, or on the boundary itself. For example, of the thirty-four Shropshire moats to be found in existing villages, seventeen are near the centre and thirteen near the boundary, and of the 107 moats in Essex thirteen are in a central position close to the parish church, fifty-two are between the parish church and the boundary, forty-one are close to the boundary, and one is on the boundary. Often the location of a moat within a settlement can tell us something of the history of that settlement. It appears that during the thirteenth century it was common for a manor house to move its site from a central position in the village to one near the edge as the village grew and the lord of the manor wanted to move away from this expansion so that he in turn had room to expand his home site. A classic example of the removal of a manor from one part of a village to another is at Wharram Percy (North Yorkshire), a deserted medieval village which has been under excavation since 1952. Here the manor house moved not once but twice to escape the progressive encroachments of the village. In villages where such movement took place there would therefore be an old and a new manor site, and where they were moated there would consequently be two moats within the same village. This takes us back to the question of dating moats, which is all-important if we are to tell whether migration of the manor house site has taken place in the village under study, with no overlap of occupation, or whether the village was divided into more than one manor, where the moats represent the sites of these manors, occupied contemporaneously.

Sometimes the peripheral position of a moat in a village is the result of the village itself moving rather than the manor house, as seems to have been the case at Acton Burnell in Shropshire. Here the moated manor site, now destroyed, began in the centre of the village, but in the latter part of the thirteenth century Acton Burnell Castle was built about 0.5 kilometre (⅓ mile) away,

Fig. 8. Distribution map of moated sites in England and Wales.

becoming the new manorial site, and the village moved closer to it, so leaving the original central moat on the perimeter of the new village location.

However, because a variety of structures were moated in the medieval period, as we shall see later, the presence of more than one moat need not *necessarily* indicate either a multiple-manor

Fig. 9. Distribution map of Welsh moated sites.

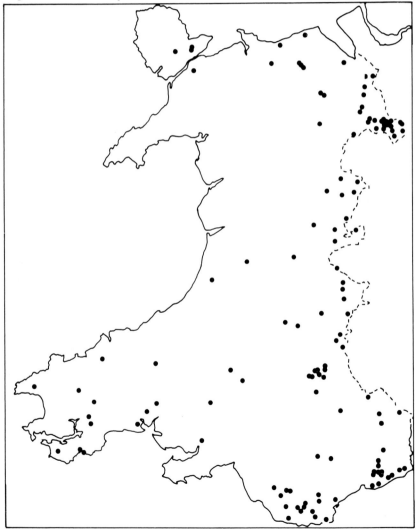

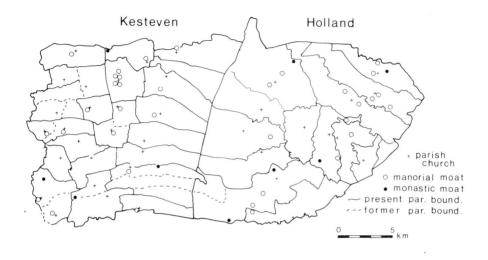

Kesteven   Holland

+ parish church
o manorial moat
• monastic moat
— present par. bound.
--- former par. bound.

0   5 km

Fig. 10. Differences in moat location in the adjacent areas of Kesteven and Holland, south Lincolnshire.

village or a change of manorial site.

The diversity and complexity of moat location within settlements is well illustrated in the ancient areas of Kesteven and Holland in south Lincolnshire (fig. 10). In the basically upland Kesteven there is commonly only one moat in each parish and it is generally in a central position close to the church. In Holland, however, which is predominantly fenland, there is often more than one moat to a parish, and when there *is* only one it does not occupy a central position. One of the complicating factors, particularly in Holland, is the presence of monastic manors and granges. From the group of south Lincolnshire parishes shown in fig. 10 it is clear that moats of these religious foundations are partially responsible for the multiplicity within parishes and that they also occupy peripheral rather than central positions.

The location of moated sites in relation to castles has not yet been studied in sufficient detail for any general conclusions to be reached, but in Essex there is a close correlation in distribution between circular moats and motte and bailey castles, and this might support the evidence obtained from excavation that circular moats belong to the early phase of moat construction.

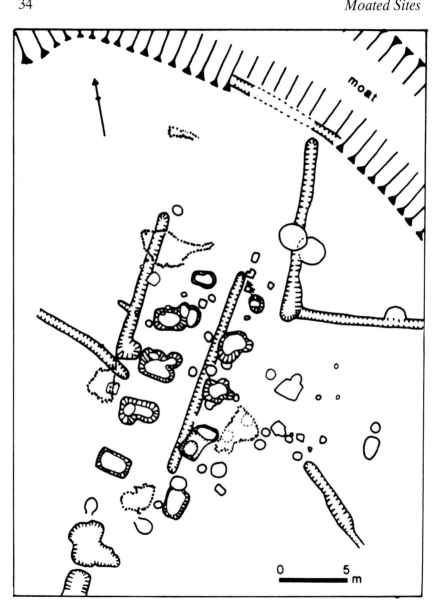

Fig. 11. Plan of superimposition of building phases on a moated site at Brome (Suffolk).

6
Buildings on moated platforms

All buildings and other stuctures within a moated area fall into two basic categories: those which have long since ceased to stand above the ground and are thus only found by excavation aided by documentary evidence, and those which are still standing, albeit sometimes in a ruinous condition.

Excavational and documentary evidence

The excavation of moated sites has been too frequently in the form of exploratory trenches, which often do little more than damage the site and lead to limited and possibly incorrect interpretations. For the early phases of medieval occupation the building evidence is often in the form of, for example, post holes which held timber uprights or slots in the ground which housed timber sills that supported uprights, and so knowledge of early structures has to be derived mainly from the relatively few moated platforms that have been excavated on a larger scale than trenching. A further limitation is that many moated sites, although probably not the majority, still have standing buildings on them, and so the platforms are not available for anything more than partial excavation. This can be a serious problem in certain areas, such as East Anglia, where there is a high proportion of moated sites still occupied.

A major problem in the excavation of moated sites, as with many other types of site, is that presented by various super-imposed and adjacent phases of occupation, where these phases have to be disentangled to provide a picture of the site as it was at any given time in its history. Sometimes the complexity that can be encountered is partly due to pre-moat activity on the site. Fig. 11 shows a not particularly complex example from Brome (Suffolk) of the superimposition of building phases, one of which predated the moat, while fig. 12 illustrates a much more complicated site, at Caldecote (Hertfordshire), where the excava-tion revealed a prehistoric beaker inhumation, iron age field boundaries, and a sequence of medieval buildings dating from the eleventh to the fifteenth century. The time scale of the features at Caldecote, because of pre-moat activity, is longer than generally occurs on a moated site, but post-moat occupation from the medieval period to the present day, with all its attendant phases of building and destruction, is common enough. A site at Buttery

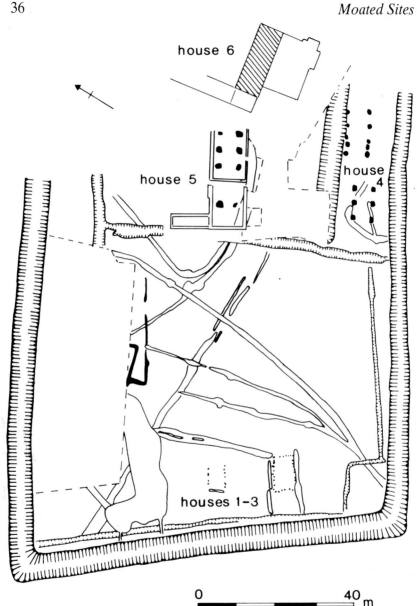

Fig. 12. Caldecote Manor (Hertfordshire), showing the complex of iron age and medieval boundaries and ditches, and medieval buildings. Houses 1-3 date from about 1050-1200, house 4 from about 1200, house 5 from about 1300 and the oldest part (shaded) of house 6 from about 1475.

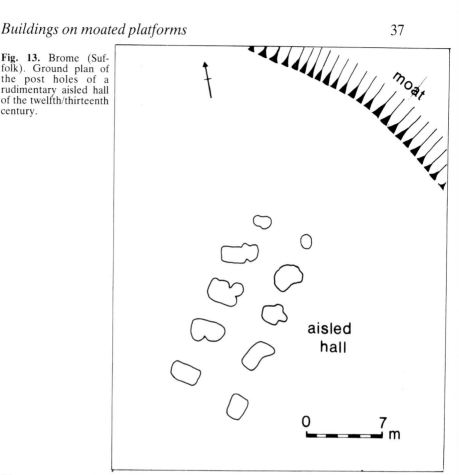

Fig. 13. Brome (Suffolk). Ground plan of the post holes of a rudimentary aisled hall of the twelfth/thirteenth century.

aisled hall

0   7 m

House Lane, Hale Barns (Greater Manchester), showed evidence of occupation from at least the thirteenth century down to the early 1950s, when the last buildings were bulldozed.

The most common medieval building for which archaeological evidence is found on a moated platform is the manor house or hall, sometimes a simple, rudimentary structure such as that suggested by the ground plan of the twelfth/thirteenth-century aisled hall with clay walls at Brome (Suffolk; fig. 13), and sometimes a much more elaborate building, such as the stone-built late thirteenth/early fourteenth-century hall at Michelham Priory (East Sussex; fig. 14), which had chalk and sandstone rubble foundations 2 metres (6 feet 7 inches) deep, buttressed walls, service areas and probably a *lavatorium*.

A particularly interesting manor house was excavated at

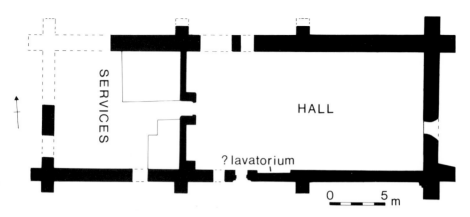

Fig. 14. Michelham Priory, Upper Dicker (East Sussex). Ground plan of the stone-built hall of the late thirteenth/early fourteenth century.

Hempstead (Norfolk), which in two of its three rooms had both decorated and undecorated medieval floor tiles (fig. 15). Such luxury is uncommon on moated sites. Some ground plans of buildings found on other sites are shown in fig. 16 a-d.

Whenever possible, attempts are made to reconstruct, usually

Fig. 15. Hempstead (Norfolk). Decorated (black) and undecorated medieval floor tiles in the moated manor.

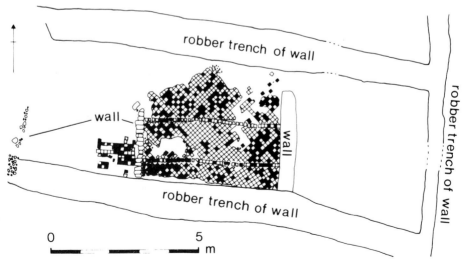

Fig. 16a. Excavated ground plan of Griff Manor House (Sudeley Castle; Gloucestershire).

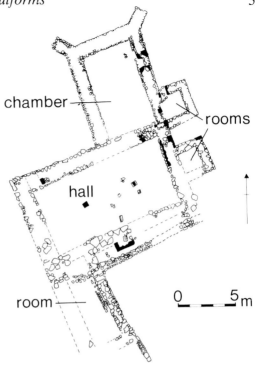

chamber

rooms

hall

room

0   5 m

Fig. 16b. Ellington Thorpe (Cambridgeshire): excavated ground plan of building.

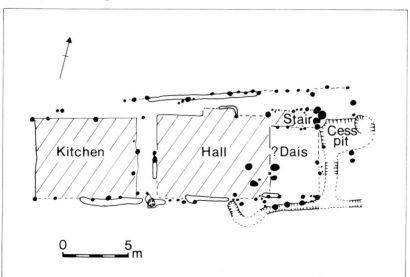

Kitchen

Hall

?Dais

Stair

Cess pit

0   5 m

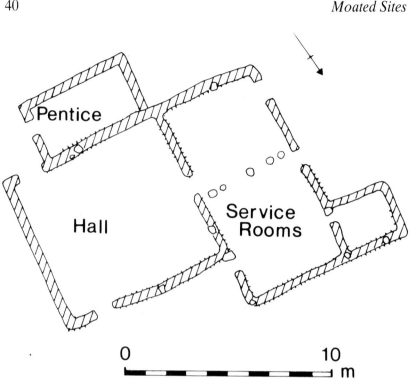

Fig. 16c. Wintringham (Cambridgeshire): excavated ground plan of building.

on paper rather than on the ground, buildings where ground plans have been determined. Fig. 17a shows the conjectured reconstruction of the mid thirteenth-century house at Wintringham (ground plan in fig. 16c), and fig. 17b is a cut-away reconstruction of a pre-moat building on the platform at East Haddlesey (North Yorkshire; ground plan in fig. 16d).

The manor house or hall is not the only building that excavation reveals. For example, at Stretham (West Sussex) the excavator found, in addition to a stone-built hall, a corn-drying oven, a timber-framed building, a retainers' hall, a kitchen and an industrial complex, dating from about 1200 to the fifteenth century. At Wintringham (Cambridgeshire) there was a house comprising a hall, cross-wing, bakehouse and pentice (a small structure attached to a larger building), and detached from the house were kitchens, bowers, a possible corn-drying building, a dovecote, provision-store buildings and another domestic build-

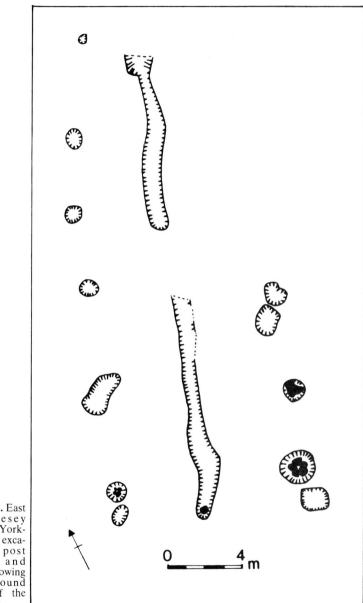

Fig. 16d. East Haddlesey (North Yorkshire): excavated post holes and slots showing the ground plan of the building.

0   4 m

ing. Indeed, buildings of this sort are not uncommonly excavated on moated sites together, very often, with a chapel, barns, stables and various other outbuildings.

On manorial sites the manor house or hall, of whatever plan and whatever construction, is always to be found, but the other buildings may or may not be present on any site, or at any particular period on a site. And excavation has shown that all buildings are likely to have changed in form and/or function during their various phases of use and occupation.

Not all excavations have produced the sorts of structures discussed above. For example, a site at Meaux, Beverley (Humberside), was a moated industrial works comprising a number of tile kilns, the earliest of which was a floor-tile kiln of the mid thirteenth century. But perhaps the oddest moated sites are those that have produced no evidence of any structures whatsoever. Sometimes it may be that poor excavation techniques are to blame for failing to recognise the fugitive remains of structures, and sometimes later activity on a site can destroy early evidence. Given these two possibilities, however, there still remain some sites that seem to have been structureless, and it may be that they were gardens, orchards or animal enclosures. For example, of a complex of four moated sites at Rickmansworth (Hertfordshire), two were excavated sufficiently to show that there were no structures on them and that they were probably gardens surrounded by fishponds.

The documentary evidence often includes lists of early buildings and other features on a moated platform. For example, a document of 1313 referring to Burgh Hall, Tuttington (Norfolk), states that repairs were needed to the value of £200 to buildings which included a great hall with various chambers, a kitchen and a larder, two chapels, watch towers, stables, barns, dairies, a bakehouse and a brewhouse. A more detailed document, an Extent of the Manor of Hodsock (Nottinghamshire) for 1324, reads: '. . . there is a certain manor, surrounded on all sides with a moat, in which are: one hall, three chambers, a pantry, a kitchen, a bakehouse, a granery, two barns, one chapel, two stables, one chamber above the bridge with portcullis and a drawbridge, one malt-kiln, two fish ponds . . . There is one garden . . . There is one dovecote.' It might seem surprising to find reference to ponds within the moated enclosure, but this is not unusual, either during the medieval period or later. One which had been filled in during the eighteenth century was found on the author's excavation at Buttery House Lane, Hale Barns (Greater Manchester).

Fig. 17a. Conjectured reconstruction of a thirteenth-century house at Wintringham (Cambridgeshire) (see fig. 16c for excavated ground plan).

Fig. 17b. Conjectured cut-away reconstruction of a pre-moat building on the platform at East Haddlesey (North Yorkshire; see fig. 16d for excavated ground plan).

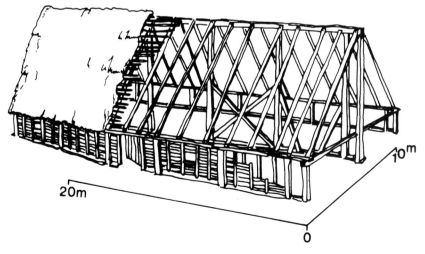

20m

10m

0

Plate 8. Stokesay Castle (Shropshire).

A document of 1429 referring to the important site of Hulme Hall, Allostock (Cheshire), lists parts of the hall and other buildings: 'the lesser chamber, le Pantre, le Buttre, the Larder, le Deyhouse, le Malthous, le . . . berne, le Hayberne, le Vyne Yorde, le Night'gale Erber, le Lytell Erber, the bridge'. An interesting inclusion in this list is the vineyard, and there is a similar reference in a lease of the Manor of Planers, Shoreham (Kent), dated 1480, which records a hall with a high dais, two ground-floor chambers at the west end, one chamber over these two and another over the larder, a kitchen, gardens, vines, a dovecote, a stable, a barn and a bridge.

Documents of this sort can be of great value to the archaeologist, helping him to recognise particular buildings from the ground plans of excavated structures, and also indicating where there were upper storeys, which are not always easily determined archaeologically.

Documents, excavation and fieldwork can indicate the *range* of structures and features that could be moated during the medieval period. Not uncommonly we find from these sources moated enclosures that were secondary to the main manorial moat, and which could contain single structures such as a chapel, a lodge, an icehouse, a windmill and even, as documented for Frodsham

Plate 9. Oxburgh Hall (Norfolk).
Plate 10. Little Moreton Hall (Cheshire).

(Cheshire), a haystack. In addition, a secondary moat could enclose an orchard or a garden. Ecclesiastical buildings (other than chapels) were often moated, and they include monastic granges, monasteries, nunneries, colleges of canons and hospitals. This range of moated structures indicates the danger of assuming that all moats were dug for the same reason.

Standing buildings

Many moated sites are still occupied and a variety of buildings, although rarely the earliest, stand on the platforms. The proper study of these buildings lies within the area of architectural history rather than that of moated sites, and therefore they will be discussed here only briefly.

Some of the most impressive buildings are to be found on those sites that received licences to crenellate, resulting in the *quasi*-castle type of fortified manor house. One striking example is Stokesay Castle (Shropshire; plate 8), which obtained a licence to crenellate in 1291. The platform has a perimeter wall, around which the remaining buildings are ranged, including the thirteenth-century great hall and two towers, one possibly twelfth-century and the other probably late thirteenth. The moat is crossed by a bridge and the platform is entered through a half-timbered sixteenth-century gatehouse.

Oxburgh Hall (Norfolk; plate 9), licensed to crenellate in 1482, is a stately example of an embattled moated structure. It is a square courtyard mansion, tightly set within the moated area, with a fine fifteenth-century brick gatehouse, flanked by octagonal turrets rising sheer from the moat to a height of 24 metres (80 feet).

Of the non-crenellated sites, Little Moreton Hall in Cheshire (plate 10 and cover) is one of the most famous. It is a courtyard house, picturesquely timber-framed in classic Cheshire black and white tradition, with its gatehouse leaning forward at such an angle that it seems likely to fall into the moat. The oldest part of the building is the Great Hall, which is late fifteenth-century, whilst the living quarters were remodelled in the sixteenth century. The courtyard and buildings occupy only one corner of a large platform. At Ightham Mote (Kent; plate 11), however, where buildings of the fourteenth century are surrounded by others of the fifteenth and sixteenth centuries, the buildings and courtyard fit tightly on to the platform, with the outer walls dropping straight down to form the inner edge of the moat. Equally integral with the moat is Birtsmorten Court (Hereford

Plate 11. Ightham Mote (Kent).
Plate 12. Birtsmorten Court (Hereford and Worcester).

Plate 13. Sinai Park, near Burton upon Trent (Staffordshire).
Plate 14. Hilton Hall (Staffordshire): a building of the eighteenth and nineteenth centuries replacing an earlier one.

and Worcester; plate 12), where the lower stone walls drop vertically into it. The court was rebuilt in about 1580 with timbers that were probably taken from an earlier building on the site, and other alterations and modifications took place down to the nineteenth century. The earliest standing structure is the four-teenth-century archway on the north side.

The moated site at Sinai Park, near Burton upon Trent (Staffordshire; plate 13), is generally considered to have been the summer residence of the Abbots of Burton, but the design of the earliest timber framing perhaps suggests a medieval hospital. Some of the buildings seem to have been dismantled and reassembled in post-medieval times to help adapt the layout to then fashionable house plans, so that in effect the medieval back of the house became the post-medieval front.

Many buildings on moated sites date from the seventeenth to the twentieth centuries, and often these buildings completely replace earlier ones (plate 14). However, it is not uncommon for later buildings to mask within them parts of earlier buildings, such as at Purshull Hall, Elmbridge (Hereford and Worcester), with its concealed cruck frame, Hulme Hall, Allostock (Cheshire), with its moulded internal beams, and Littywood (Staffordshire), where a medieval cruck-framed open hall is disguised by a building of the nineteenth and twentieth centuries.

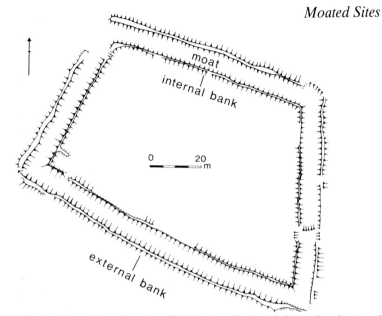

Fig. 18. Hartley Court Moat, Burnham (Buckinghamshire), with internal and external banks.

Fig. 19. Evington Moat (Leicestershire). Moated site with a series of medieval fishponds.

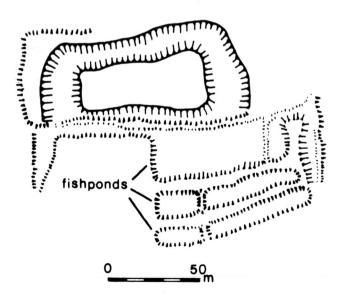

7
Associated features

On and adjacent to moated sites there are often earthworks and features such as earthen banks, fishponds and other water systems, and generally these have received far less attention from excavators than have the platforms. In addition, many of these features have virtually disappeared because of levelling and infilling. As a result knowledge of them is limited.

Internal and external banks are not uncommon on moated sites (see fig. 18), and it is tempting to consider them as defensive, but without excavation, and sometimes even after excavation, it is difficult to determine their purpose. If post or stake holes are found in the tops of these banks, then we may well have the evidence for the timber uprights of some sort of defensive fence or palisade; unfortunately, this evidence has seldom been forthcoming, two exceptions being Weoley Castle, Birmingham, where the earliest phases, from about 1150 to about 1260, were marked by a ditch with an internal bank, in the top of which were the post holes of a possible palisade (see fig. 4), and Shifnal (Shropshire), where excavation located a timber palisade on the inner bank of the platform. A further and unusual exception was a site at Llys Edwin, in the old county of Flintshire (now Clwyd), where excavation showed evidence of a palisade of sharpened stakes on an external bank, and part of the palisade itself was found charred in the moat. In all of the cases where excavation has revealed no such holes, then either the bank has been so eroded that the holes have been entirely removed, or else it was in no way defensive but was simply the result of dumping material from the digging or scouring of the moat.

Also, if no excavation has taken place to prove or disprove it, then an internal bank running around the edge of the platform could be a build-up of soil and turf overlying a collapsed or robbed perimeter wall.

Outside the moated area there is frequently evidence of medieval water systems of various kinds, the most common being fishponds. In some cases there is only one pond, but often there is a series, such as at Evington Moat, Leicester (fig. 19). Much more complex water systems are found at some sites: at Durrance Moat, Upton Warren (Hereford and Worcester), for example, there is an intricate arrangement of dams, ponds, natural and artificial watercourses (fig. 20), and the use of leats to carry water to and from moats is a feature of many sites throughout Britain.

Moated sites should not be considered in isolation, but as part of a larger pattern probably exemplified at its largest, archaeologically, by the abandoned manorial moat lying within its deserted

Fig. 20. Complex medieval water system at Durrance Moat, Upton Warren (Hereford and Worcester).

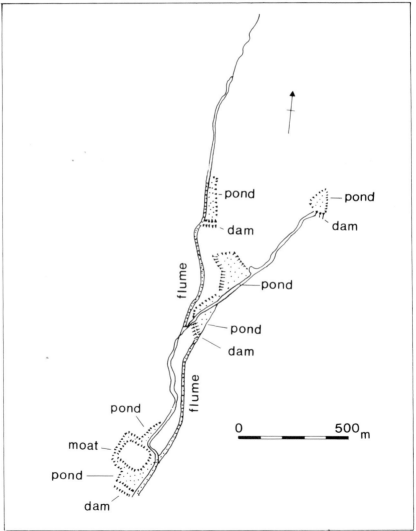

Plate 15. Wormleighton (Warwickshire): abandoned moat lying within the deserted medieval village.

medieval village, the existence of which is indicated by the humps of house platforms and the hollows of streets and boundaries (plate 15).

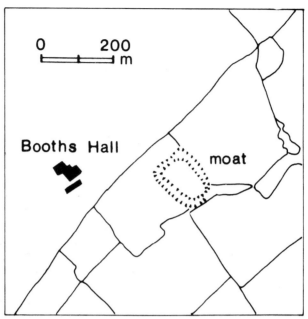

Fig. 21. The deserted moated site of the original Booths Hall, Knutsford (Cheshire), and the new (1745) Booths Hall 200 metres (656 feet) away.

Plate 16. Park House, Gainsborough (Lincolnshire): filled-in and ploughed-out moated complex now showing only as crop marks.

8
Desertion of moated sites

Many moated sites today are totally deserted, with no standing buildings on the platform and with the moat itself often overgrown. The reasons for desertion can vary from site to site but one of the most common is simply that there came a time when a moat was no longer needed or fashionable, and it became a nuisance, an eyesore, or too restricting. As a result, one of three things could be done: the moat could be filled in; it could be drained and landscaped; or the buildings on the platform could be pulled down and new ones built some distance from the moated area, so leaving the original site deserted. This abandoning of moats was particularly common in the seventeenth and eighteenth centuries with the building of the great halls and country houses, and the evidence is clearly shown on present-day maps, where a hall, or 'New Hall' as it is sometimes called, is often located up to a mile away from a deserted moated site, occasionally marked as 'site of Old Hall' (fig. 21).

Desertion could take place earlier than the seventeenth century, for a variety of reasons. Not uncommonly, it could happen because the settlement in which it was situated was abandoned, either moving site or ceasing to exist at all. The moated site at Wintringham (Cambridgeshire) moved, with its hamlet, from a low-lying position to a higher one in about 1340, leaving the original settlement site and moat deserted. A more unusual example is that of Foxtwist, near Macclesfield (Cheshire), which took place in 1358. The owner of the 'Hall and Chamber' on this moated site, Robert de Foxwist, fell out of favour with the Black Prince, was exiled and apparently the hall was dismantled, taken to Macclesfield and re-erected as the town hall.

One consequence of moated sites becoming deserted is that they may 'disappear': the platform can be levelled and the moat filled in, as has happened extensively in the nineteenth and twentieth centuries with the increasing demand for agricultural and building land (plate 16). As a result of moats vanishing, it is difficult to be sure how many originally existed, but fieldwork, documents, maps and aerial photography have revealed many 'lost' sites.

9
European moated sites

The study of moated sites began even later on the continent of Europe than it did in Britain, and so knowledge of them is limited and uneven. The evidence that we have from those few areas where research has been done suggests that earthworks similar to those found in Britain are a common feature of areas of north-western Europe.

The area of densest concentration so far recorded is in Flanders, where no village has fewer than ten moats per square kilometre, which exceeds the number found in any equivalent area of Britain. The regions of the Netherlands are also well represented, with just under one hundred in Utrecht, about fifty in the Betuwe, and quite high numbers in Groningen, Friesland and the County of Holland, although the actual figures have not yet been determined. They are also very common in France and are a fairly typical feature of rural north-west Germany and to a lesser extent of Denmark. In Poland the numbers vary in different parts of the country, the two densest areas being Silesia, where there are more than four hundred, and Great Poland, where there are about 150. However, for reasons that are mentioned later, Polish sites are slightly outside the terms of reference of this book.

From hardly any areas do we have anything more than superficial information regarding the physical nature of moated sites and their associations. In Flanders they are mainly square or rectangular, with some examples of double moats, and there seems to be a development in platform types from the twelfth century, when the platforms were raised 3 to 4 metres (10 to 13 feet) above the surrounding area, to the fourteenth century, when they were barely raised at all. The moats are never less than 8 to 10 metres (26 to 33 feet) wide, and sometimes reach a width of 23 metres (75 feet). In the Burgundy region of France, the platforms are usually rectangular and sometimes slightly raised, and excavation of one site showed that the moat was 12 metres (39 feet) wide and 3 metres (10 feet) deep. In north-west Germany the moated area can be either round, oval or rectangular, with the sides varying in length from 50 to 80 metres (164 to 262 feet) and the moat from 5 to 8 metres (16 to 26 feet) wide. Polish sites do not appear to be quite of the sort that we are dealing with: they are usually mounds with a diameter of 30 to 40 metres (98 to 131 feet), surrounded by a wall or bank and by a moat, and originally supporting a timber tower. Consequently they seem much more like mottes than the moated sites of our definition, and their military nature is indicated by the artefacts that excavations have produced, including parts of crossbows, battleaxes and spearheads.

As in Britain, European moats can be situated either centrally in a village, or some distance away from the centre, or outside the settlement, but sometimes factors peculiar to an area will have determined the position. For example, in the province of Utrecht in the Netherlands hardly any sites are situated in a settlement, whereas in the neighbouring Betuwe they are nearly all within villages, usually peripheral, and the reason for this probably lies in differences in the patterns of early land reclamation between the two areas.

The possession of a moat in Europe, again as in Britain, is commonly a mark of status and is associated with particular social classes. In the County of Holland the moat was the hallmark of a freeman, especially a member of the knightly class, and the same is generally true for the rest of the Netherlands, although in the Groningen-Friesland region there are also moated farms, about which virtually nothing is known. The *maison fort* was a very widespread feature of medieval France from the thirteenth century onwards and was a relatively modest moated manorial site owned by the local lord. The late medieval manor house sites of Denmark are similar in form to British moated sites, but most of them are of superior social status; they were built by prominent nobility and the buildings on them frequently reflect this. Some later, smaller versions of these sites may have had a similar social status to those in England. In Flanders some moats belonged to monasteries, but most are associated with small farmsteads, and it seems likely that most medieval farms held by freeholders had a moat. Indeed, the high incidence of moats in the coastal areas is probably because there were more freehold farmers here than elsewhere in Flanders. In Jutland, where they probably date from the fifteenth or sixteenth century, and in north-west Germany, where they mostly date from the twelfth to fifteenth centuries, moated farms are also common and they were probably owned by a class of farmer similar to that of Flanders, although evidence from Jutland is very thin.

The standing buildings on European moated sites are generally late, and there has been so little excavation that there are few general statements that we can make about early or original

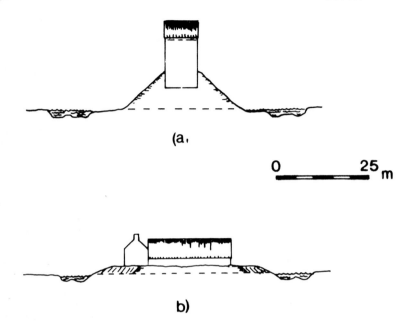

Fig. 22. Profiles of a moated site at Zwartewaal (Holland): (a) in 1250; (b) in 1400.

buildings. From this limited excavation, and from documentary sources, it is clear that farm buildings were not uncommon on sites and domestic buildings of varying status are usual. For example, near Rotterdam a thirteenth-century moated site contained a brick barn with a bakehouse, while documents from Burgundy record living quarters and farm buildings together on the same site, and an excavation within the region produced remains of a timber hall 20 metres (66 feet) by 9.5 metres (31 feet). In Denmark the late medieval moated sites frequently contained a stately, elaborate, several-winged manor house.

One type of building, found only occasionally in Britain but much more often in Europe, is the tower, which has been recorded both in excavations and in documents. In Burgundy towers are usually rectangular and made of stone and share the moated platform with the domestic and farm buildings. In northern Germany the towers, either of timber or stone, functioned as store houses, but in Holland they were the living accommodation of knights, from the thirteenth century onwards, originally being sited on a motte, and later built on a flat surface surrounded by a moat which might also include farm buildings, although these might be within a separate moat (fig. 22). Two excavations from Holland have produced evidence relating to towers. On one site, at Oosterwijk, a platform 24 metres (79 feet) by 27 metres (89 feet) contains evidence of a domestic building and was enclosed by a wall which had a tower set in one of the inner corners. This complex seems to date from about 1400 and it replaced a thirteenth-century tower which had been pulled down in 1351. The other excavation, at Poortugaal, was on a site which was a twelfth-century replacement of an earlier site and which comprised a small platform, 8 by 8 metres (26 by 26 feet), surrounded by a substantial moat 10 metres (33 feet) wide, and supporting a wooden tower, which in about 1220 was replaced by a brick one. Some of these western European 'tower sites' were probably similar in purpose to those of Poland, but in the main they appear to have been minimally defensive and mainly a display of status.

Scholars in various European countries are working on the problems of moated sites, but until their research, both documentary and archaeological, bears fruit knowledge of these sites is necessarily patchy and thin and does not permit the making of valid comparisons and contrasts between British and European moated sites.

10
Further reading

There are no general books devoted solely to moated sites, but a list is given below of books and journals where they are discussed. The first in the list is a specialist research report containing various contributions by different authors.

Aberg, F. A. (editor). *Medieval Moated Sites*. Council for British Archaeology Research Report 17, 1978.
Atkins, P. V. 'Medieval Moated Sites'. *Amateur Historian* 10, 1972.
Cantor, L. C. (editor). *The English Medieval Landscape*. Croom Helm, 1982.
Emery, F. V. 'Moated Settlements in England'. *Geography* 47, 1962.
Fowler, P. J. (editor). *Archaeology and the Landscape*. John Baker, 1972.
Le Patourel, J. *The Moated Sites of Yorkshire*. Society for Medieval Archaeology Monograph number 5, 1973.
Platt, C. *Medieval England*. Routledge and Kegan Paul, 1978.
Roberts, B. K. 'Moated Sites'. *Amateur Historian* 5.2, 1962.

The Moated Sites Research Group publishes a report each year, dealing with both local and wider aspects, and county archaeological journals often contain details of moat excavations. People interested in learning more about the work of the Moated Sites Research Group should contact the Secretary, 29 Pine Walk, Liss, Hampshire GU33 7AT.

11
Moated sites to visit

The times when these sites are open to the public vary and intending visitors are advised to check before making a special journey. Many other sites, on farm land, can be reached by footpath or by permission of the landowner.

Baddesley Clinton, Knowle, Solihull, West Midlands B93 0DQ. Telephone: Lapworth (056 43) 3294. Grid reference: SP 199722.

Broughton Castle, Broughton, Banbury, Oxfordshire OX15 5EB. Telephone: Banbury (0295) 62624. Grid reference: SP 416384.

Great Chalfield Manor, Melksham, Wiltshire SN12 8NH. Grid reference: ST 860630.

Hales Hall, Loddon, Norwich, Norfolk. Grid reference: TG 368961.

Harvington Hall, Harvington, Kidderminster, Worcestershire DY10 4LR. Grid reference: SO 877745.

Ightham Mote, Ivy Hatch, Sevenoaks, Kent. Telephone: Sevenoaks (0732) 62235. Grid reference: TQ 584535.

Kentwell Hall, Long Melford, Sudbury, Suffolk CO10 9BA. Grid reference: TL 863479.

Little Moreton Hall, Congleton, Cheshire. Telephone: Congleton (026 02) 72018. Grid reference: SJ 832589.

Lower Brockhampton, Bromyard, Herefordshire. Telephone: Bromyard (0885) 2258. Grid reference: SO 682546.

Mannington Hall, Saxthorpe, Norwich, Norfolk NR11 7BB. Telephone: Saxthorpe (026 387) 284. Grid reference: TG 144320.

Markenfield Hall, Ripon, North Yorkshire HG4 3AD. Grid reference: SE 294673.

Michelham Priory, Upper Dicker, Hailsham, East Sussex BN23 3QS. Telephone: Hailsham (0323) 844224. Grid reference: TQ 558093.

Newtimber Place, Newtimber, Hassocks, West Sussex BN6 9BU. Telephone: Hurstpierpoint (0273) 833104. Grid reference: TQ 268137.

Oakwell Hall, Birstall, Batley, West Yorkshire. Telephone: Batley (0924) 474926. Grid reference: SE 218271.

Otley Hall, Otley, Ipswich, Suffolk. Grid reference: TM 207563.

Oxburgh Hall, Oxborough, King's Lynn, Norfolk PE33 9PS.
  Telephone: Gooderstone (036 621) 258. Grid reference: TF
  742012.
Stokesay Castle, Stokesay, Craven Arms, Shropshire. Telephone: Craven Arms (058 82) 2544. Grid reference: SO
  436817.

Index